SENSITIVITY of HEART

HOW TO BE SENSITIVE

TO THE FATHER,

HIS WORD AND

ONE ANOTHER

Kenneth Copeland

KENNETH COPELAND
PUBLICATIONS

TABLE OF

Contents

CHAPTER ONE

Sensitivity
of
Heart

Sensitivity of Heart

You and I are privileged to be part of the most unique generation in Church history. We are at the crossroads of the two most important ages in the history of this planet. Six thousand years of human history have come to a close. The millennial reign of Jesus of Nazareth is about to open. The conflict between heaven and hell is coming together. Soon, Satan will be removed for the first time from human contact since the Garden of Eden and the authority of Almighty God re-established in the earth. All the things God ever said He would do—we're about to witness their fulfillment. We have the privilege and responsibility of being pioneers in this unique time in history. Time is giving birth to a new era and the labor pains are part of the last moments of the last days.

The pains are more constant now. The Body of Christ is under more pressure than ever before. Satan's time is short and he knows it. He is trying everything he can think of to put pressure on the Church to stop us from accomplishing our task.

The Word and our faith are meeting more resistance than ever before. But let me encourage you—it's not a tragedy to live in this generation. Your birth into the earth was not untimely. You are right on time. You are right where you belong! If you and I did not have what it takes to make it in this generation, God would have had us born at another time.

You are right where you belong!

Our generation will see the fulfillment of all things. We will introduce the next age through the signs and wonders of Almighty God and manifestations of the Holy Spirit. We will be participants in the greatest works of the Holy Spirit the human race has ever seen.

We must become sensitive to the Spirit of

God in order to bring His love and power to the lost and dying of this world for whom Jesus shed His precious blood, and to usher in His glory. Because of His Anointing on us and in us, millions of people will be healed, delivered and swept into the kingdom of God as we develop our sensitivity to hear and obey the Holy Spirit.

CHAPTER TWO

Insensitivity to God

Insensitivity to God

Though God Himself was living among them, the Pharisees were insensitive to the Holy Spirit. Mark 3 speaks of a time when Jesus and His disciples went into the synagogue. There, the Pharisees watched and waited, trying to accuse Him of some violation of their traditions.

Mark 3:1-3 says, "And he entered again into the synagogue; and there was a man there which had a withered hand. And they watched him, whether he would heal him on the sabbath day; that they might accuse him. And he saith unto the man which had the withered hand, Stand forth." Or as the *Amplified Bible, Classic Edition* says, "Get up [and stand here] in the midst." Jesus brought the man right out

in the middle to be seen, knowing that everyone there wanted to accuse Him.

> And he saith unto them, Is it lawful
> to do good on the sabbath days, or to do
> evil? to save life, or to kill? But they
> held their peace. And when he had
> looked round about on them with anger,
> being grieved for the hardness of their
> hearts, he saith unto the man, Stretch
> forth thine hand. And he stretched it
> out: and his hand was restored whole as
> the other. And the Pharisees went forth,
> and straightway took counsel with the
> Herodians against him, how they might
> destroy him. But Jesus withdrew himself
> with his disciples to the sea (verses 4-7).

When Jesus questioned the Pharisees according to the will and purpose of God, they said
nothing. He looked on them with anger because
of their hardness of heart—or insensitivity.

They were insensitive to who was in their
midst, not realizing that it was God. They, of all
people, should have known the Scriptures. Jesus
fit every Messianic prophecy. But they had made

traditions from the Word and had stepped over into esteeming their traditions more than God.

We tend to look down on them, but we have all done the same thing. We, too, have had a "form of godliness, but denying the power thereof" (2 Timothy 3:5). The reason is insensitivity. We have not been sensitive to the Spirit of God nor to the magnitude of the price God Almighty paid for our redemption. This kind of attitude angered Jesus.

Thank God, His anger is but for a moment. We have preached it as though His anger were forever and His mercy but for a moment. I have determined I will preach, "his mercy endureth *for ever*" (1 Chronicles 16:34). Lamentations 3:23 says His mercies are new every morning.

In this situation, Jesus was angry because the Spirit of God was grieved. I have experienced that grief in my own ministry. It has happened a few times while ministering in prayer lines as God's Spirit was moving. Suddenly, a grieving of the Holy Spirit that cannot be adequately explained in words came up inside me. It was the heaviest grief I have ever sensed.

The Apostle Paul in Ephesians 4:30

admonishes us to "grieve not the holy Spirit of God, whereby ye are sealed unto the day of redemption." Why?

To minister effectively, one must have the Anointing of God. Therefore, I must yield myself totally to His Spirit. When I am a yielded vessel to Him, I see through His eyes and hear through His ears. My spirit molds together with the Holy Spirit. My emotions are one with His. I am moved and directed as He is moved. When He is grieved I am grieved and His Anointing lifts. When that happens, I am helpless as a bird without wings. I cannot minister without His Anointing.

To minister effectively, one must have the Anointing of God.

When the anointing stops flowing, burdens and yokes remain. People are unchanged. God's heart is for His people to be set free. So when His Anointing stops flowing, grief becomes like fire down on the inside of my innermost being. I want to know what has caused it. A holy anger comes over me. The first few times that happened I felt condemned for feeling that way.

In one of my meetings, I started to lay my

hands on a young woman and she began shaking her head and crying, "No, no, no!" When I laid my hands on her, nothing happened.

I started to walk away thinking, *There are several hundred people here to minister to. I don't have time to preach to her until I get faith to rise up in her heart.* For a moment I just prayed in the spirit. As I prayed, grief and anger rose up on the inside of me. It came from deep down in my spirit. But, the Spirit of God was in control. I took her face in my hands and in a firm voice I said, "Don't you say no to me. I am here in the Name of Almighty God as His prophet to set you free." She looked up at me and batted her eyes a few times. It startled me as much as it did her. I began to weep from the very depths of my being. The flow of God's compassion through me broke the power of that evil spirit and she received from God.

This gives you some indication of what must have been inside Jesus that day in the synagogue. He was grieved because the hardness of the Pharisees' hearts quenched the Anointing of God. The word translated *hardness* means "insensitiveness." It is translated in other scriptures as "blindness."

The Pharisees were insensitive to God. When we read this, it is easy to imagine a group of hardened people who were angry enough to kill. But it doesn't take that high level of insensitivity to quench the Holy Spirit. God is love. He yearns to manifest that love. When we are hardhearted and insensitive toward others, it grieves Him.

The Pharisees look bad to us. And that situation was openly hard, but an act of insensitivity can be something that may seem insignificant to us.

I remember a particular instance when I was ministering in a prayer service and God was moving tremendously. The power of God was so strong that it twice drained the battery in the wireless microphone I was wearing!

Why did Jesus withdraw? Because without the Anointing of God He couldn't do anything. And if He couldn't, I certainly can't.

When I reached the rear of the congregation, suddenly the anointing stopped. It was just as though the Spirit of God withdrew from the situation.

Did you notice that our scriptural example tells of a similar situation? It says, "The Pharisees…took counsel…how they might destroy him. But Jesus withdrew himself with his disciples to the sea." Why did Jesus just get up and walk off? Surely the man with the withered hand was not the only one who needed deliverance. Because without the Anointing of God He couldn't do anything. And if He couldn't, I certainly can't.

It's my nature to try it anyway. I desire for people to be healed and delivered so badly that I want to continue praying. However, it's useless when the Spirit is grieved. Without Him, nothing can be done. In the same way Jesus withdrew that day from the synagogue, He withdrew while I was ministering.

We had grieved the Spirit of God. I said, "Lord, what has happened here? Whatever it is, I repent now. Tell me what it is."

I began pleading my case as fast as I could. "Lord, look at all these people in such need. You said without You we can do nothing." I reminded myself of my daughter Kellie when she was a little girl. When she was disobedient and I would start to spank her she would turn into a "motor mouth"! "Daddy, wait a minute now, Daddy, wait a minute. I don't want you to do something you will regret. Can't we work this out? Daddy, can't we pray about it first?" She would talk me right out of it before I could spank her! It wouldn't be long before she had *me* feeling guilty because I was reprimanding *her!*

This was the way I was talking to the Lord. He answered, *Look back there at the book table.*

This particular auditorium did not have a foyer. My staff had set up the book tables inside the auditorium. I have given absolute, strict orders in our meetings that the book tables be shut down when anyone is ministering or any-time the Spirit of God is moving. The workers had covered the book tables to indicate they were closed. Someone had lifted the cover, picked out some books and expected to be waited on. My employees were not about to wait on them. That is a quick way to become unemployed at Kenneth Copeland Ministries! They know better than to compete with the Spirit of God. Two of the people were angry because no one would take their money. We

find in Ephesians 3-5 that corrupt communica-
tion, *strife* and stealing grieve the Lord.

At first, I became angry because their
insensitivity grieved the Holy Spirit and
arrested the anointing. It departed just like
Jesus departed from the synagogue. I repented
and reprimanded the congregation. In no
uncertain terms, they wanted the anointing
back and became serious with God in a hurry.
The anointing did come back but not at the
level it had been.

Another situation happened almost exactly
the same way. I was ministering the Word of
God and the power of God was so heavy you
could almost cut it with a knife. I was just about
to begin ministering in the gifts of the Spirit.
God was ready to expose the devil and drive
him out of there.

Right at that crucial moment, a dear woman
sitting second row, center got up and walked
out of the auditorium. In a few minutes she
came back with a carton full of sodas, hot dogs,
hamburgers and popcorn. The disruption dis-
tracted the congregation from being brought to
a sensitive place in God.

The woman was not being sensitive to the people who needed Jesus and salvation. She was thinking of her own needs and was not sensitive to the fact that God Almighty was at work in that place.

Jesus said, "If you receive the one whom I send, you receive Me. And if you receive Me, you receive the One who sent Me." Receiving a minister of the gospel as an anointed vessel of God, with the same respect and honor you would give Jesus, releases great power and anointing to heal and deliver. Many times, God has instructed me to tell someone I was sent and anointed by God. That is not bragging, it is faith. God uses men and women who are operating in faith. A spiritual law was at work in that meeting. By her actions, the woman was being insensitive to Jesus' instructions to honor the minister of God.

Jesus operated in the power of God because He operated in faith.

Jesus operated in the power of God because He operated in faith. He said, "I have come not to do My will, but the will of My Father who sent Me." Jesus was doing the will of God in the synagogue. The Pharisees were insensitive to who was in their midst, to the Spirit of the living God who was in operation there and to the man who needed healing. As soon as he was healed, the Pharisees left. They didn't even wait for the last "amen" or congratulate the man for receiving a miracle from God.

You will find this attitude all the way through the ministry of Jesus. There was an insensitive crowd around Him most of the time. He could do no mighty works in His own hometown because they didn't believe what He preached. They didn't care that He came to bring deliverance to the blind, to bind up the brokenhearted and to heal the sick.

Healing was the covenant right of the woman who had been bowed over for 18 years. She was a daughter of Abraham. Yet the Pharisees never ministered to her. As often as she came to services, they were more interested in their traditions than in her need.

Do you remember the blind man whom the religious leaders brought up before the council? They said of Jesus, "We know that this man is a sinner" (John 9:24). They pestered the man about Jesus until he became tired of it. He finally said, "What if I tell you *again,* will that make you believe? I was blind and now I can see. Is there some crime in being healed?" You would think so, when you are around people who have no sensitivity. They may be full of pity, or even a little sympathy, but pity and sympathy are human emotions. I'm talking about having a heart sensitive to God, and sensitive enough to others to meet their needs.

A sensitive heart is one in which the compassion of God is moving. Jesus was moved by compassion, not just sympathy. What are you moved by?

An insensitive person will leave a church service in the middle of an invitation to the lost or walk out in the middle of ministry to the sick. They'll think, *Well, I'm tired. I have to get the children to school in the morning.* It doesn't matter to them that there are people with serious needs being ministered to by the Spirit of God. Some are life and death matters. Insensitive people are moved by their selfish desires.

When believers come together, their power and strength in the spiritual realm is not only doubled, it multiplies their faith to the *10th* power. One can put 1,000 to flight, two can put 10,000 to flight. That means when someone leaves during ministry to the oppressed, there are at least 9,000 demons left unhindered because one believer stops adding his faith. Someone who remained in the service will have to take up that selfish person's part.

CHAPTER THREE

Sensitivity
to God

Sensitivity to God

I am often astounded to watch a reserved section of an auditorium full of preachers and VIPs. Many times, everyone in the congregation is dancing before the Lord and worshiping God, while the ministers and leaders have big frowns on their faces and are wondering what is going on. In this critical hour in history, as shepherds, we must be more sensitive to God and be an example to the sheep.

Most people are not as harsh as the Pharisees, but are still insensitive to the Holy Spirit. Though the Pharisees left immediately, others were still watching Jesus to accuse Him. No one in the crowd was healed but the man with the withered arm. No one.

Why do you suppose the entire synagogue full of people was insensitive enough to grieve the Holy Spirit? Because their ministers were insensitive to God. They followed their shepherds into strife, criticism and insensitivity.

As ministers of the gospel, it doesn't matter how long we have been preaching, how closely we walk in the Word or how deep our prayer life is. We cannot become satisfied with what we have already done. All we have done isn't enough. We must reach for more.

God forgives sin but He does not condone it.

We must enlarge our hearts and reach out to God. We must bathe ourselves deeply in the sensitiveness of the Holy Spirit, thinking about one another instead of ourselves. When we do, sensitivity of heart will begin to grow in our congregations.

Let's reach higher than our differences in the Body of Christ and become more sensitive to God and to the needs of others. Reach out to one another. Look for opportunities to help your brother. Look for ways to be of service to others. Seek ways to help. Be willing to give the

Word of God, in His compassion, to those who do not have as much revelation knowledge as you have been blessed with.

Sensitivity
of Speech

4

Sensitivity of Speech

As believers, we should make the decision to become sensitive to the words we speak. Our words bind us to one another. Our ability to speak makes us like God. God spoke His Word and will not change. He gave authority over the earth to Adam, and Adam gave it to the devil. God stuck by His Word though it cost Him His Son. No other being on earth but man has the right to choose words and speak them in faith.

It's time we as Christians remember the covenants we make, even if we have to swear to our own hurt. We have broken too many contracts thinking it was all right because the *other* party was not honoring it.

When we make a covenant and say, "I will,"

"I do," "I shall," "I'll be there on time," we had better honor those commitments. Until we learn to become sensitive to the integrity of our own word, we will not understand what it means to act on God's Word. His power comes from keeping His Word and it manifests in our lives as we believe and act on it. Without knowing this, it is almost impossible to grow spiritually and experience the better things of God.

God's power manifests in our lives as we believe and act on His Word.

This is why so many marriages are failing. People are insensitive to the covenant they have made. They say, "I do," and forget about it 15 minutes later. Couples who begin having trouble in their marriages should know the Bible marriage vows so well, the very moment strife comes in, they run to the Communion table. If they would get on their knees and reaffirm the covenant they made before God, reciting their vows to one another, they would find themselves as tender with one another as they were on their wedding night.

If you say, "But Brother Copeland, we are

too far gone," you've just admitted that you are too selfish to even try. Many think adultery is the major cause of divorce, but Jesus said the rite of divorcement was given "because of the hardness [or insensitiveness] of your hearts" (Matthew 19:7-8). The Body of Christ must act like God, swearing to our own hurt, where marriage is concerned. It will cause us to be as victorious as God. He is not a loser.

When you, your wife and children become sensitive to each other's needs, rather than your own, no sin on earth is big enough to stop the love of God from flowing in your household. The love of God never fails. Your marriage will not fail when it is based on God's love.

The love of God never fails.

God is moving in this hour. His eyes are searching to and fro across the earth seeking those who have a perfect heart, to whom He may show Himself strong (2 Chronicles 16:9). A "perfect heart" is a sensitive heart, one that has matured in sensitivity to God, to the needs of those around it and to the Word of God.

CHAPTER FIVE

Sensitivity
to Spiritual
Warfare

Sensitivity to Spiritual Warfare

There is a great battle going on in the earth. This war in the spirit will be fought much like wars fought in the natural. Our military works effectively through chain of command. In God's army, God is the Commander in Chief and Jesus is the Chief of Staff. We have to be sensitive to their instructions.

Training for battle takes a long time and millions of dollars. A fighter plane has a three- or four-hour range per mission. You can push that aircraft to its total capability in battle in three and one half hours. Yet, it took more than 18 months to teach the pilot how to do it. It takes more than a year to train a U.S. Marine infantryman. But real hand-to-hand combat may be over in minutes. The training takes a lot longer than the actual battle.

In the Body of Christ, we have been in training for the greatest spiritual invasion of this age. We have had skirmishes in the spiritual realm in individual lives, in local churches and in ministries. But on January 1, 1983, God began to rally and marshal His forces into one massive spiritual invasion of the strongholds of the devil. Many Christians have been fighting in a holding action for a long time, but it is time for an all-out offensive.

Do you realize that for the first time in history, God has Satan's forces split on two fronts? On one side is Israel and on the other, the Body of Christ. Satan has never been powerful enough to handle either of us alone. Now, he is faced with both of us.

The Lord said to me in mid-January 1983, in a time of prayer, *I liken this to the invasion of Europe in 1944 and '45.* It took a long time to activate that invasion because it was so massive. It had never been attempted before in human history. The free countries of the world met together in the British Isles with one goal before them: to rid the world of Adolf Hitler and all he stood for.

The Lord showed it to me this way so I could understand His position. If we understand His position in this final conflict, we can understand our own.

January 1, 1983, gave birth to a total change of spiritual atmosphere all over this world. It will continue to change. We will continue to face what no other Christian generation has ever faced, just as no other military organization in the world had ever faced an army like the one gathered in England in 1944-45. There were many new things that had to be learned.

> *We will continue to face what no other Christian generation has ever faced.*

Our generation is launching into the greatest outpouring of the Spirit of God that has ever occurred in the history of the world. This is not just maneuvers or training, nor will battles be fought individually by single churches, families or individual believers. We are coming together as the army of Jesus with one goal—to rid the earth of Satan and all he stands for! It is the final conflict when Satan will be slammed down from his position forever (Revelation 12:10).

We have some fresh troops just coming in off the street who don't know anything about religious tradition. They've not been told they can't do what the Word says they can do. Just the thought of it thrills me! Watch them. They will raise the dead before we get a chance to tell them they had better "use wisdom." Be sensitive to them. A good commander can teach and train someone who has some wildfire. He can be handled with the power and wisdom of the Holy Ghost. It's the ones who won't take action that you can't do anything with.

We also have some old "bomber crews" who have a lot of missions under their belts. They'll have their part in this invasion force. They are the ones with the experience, but some have developed a few bad habits. They got away with some things in these little missions that won't work on this big one. Those experienced troops will have to become *very* sensitive. It is often difficult to tell someone who has been successful on 30 missions that they haven't been doing it right.

Things are different now. In training they use blanks. But this enemy is for real. The devil has his guns loaded and has launched his attacks, trying to stop our invasion. He is moving in every area, attacking families like never before. Those who thought they would never contemplate divorce have started playing with those thoughts. Those who never thought about adultery are now toying with the idea. They rationalize it because they feel that suddenly, no one understands them anymore.

Some who thought they'd never see the day a glass of alcohol would come near their lips, are having a little wine with their meals and looking forward to the next glass. Believers are using foul language, words they thought would never come out of their mouths again since making Jesus the Lord of their lives.

Ministers are being bombarded with thoughts of defeat and despair. Pastors of churches who stand up for the integrity of the uncompromised Word of God are finding themselves in situations where men of God don't have any business being.

Have you noticed that Christians have

stopped calling sin, *sin?* They're calling it
their "problem" or "issue." "Well, you see I
have this problem" or "I have issues that are
really just more than I can handle, and I know
God understands."

God forgives sin but He does not condone
it. It doesn't matter what kind of problem or
issue you have, you don't have any business
getting involved with other women. I don't
care if your wife ran off because you started
talking in tongues. Even if she has lived with

another man since she left.
That doesn't mean you have
such a problem that adultery
will cure it. Adultery will not
cure it. Adultery will kill you.

> *God forgives sin but He does not condone it.*

The wages of sin is death. Sin is not the cure.
Sin is *sin.*

I know I am being blunt, but there isn't time
for sweet-talk. The devil is bloodthirsty. He'll
kill you if you let him. Training camp is over.
We have to get honest and open with one
another. We are not fighting little skirmishes
here and there. The lives of men and women all
over this world are in our hands. There is only a

short time remaining. Playtime is over.

Things we got away with a year ago, we'll not get away with now—and survive. We'll find ourselves standing knee-deep in more hell than we know how to deal with.

We have some new crews joining our forces that will have to take some crash courses in faith, love and power. It's time to act like soldiers, tighten up and get back to the Manual. We have to get back in the Word of God and become sensitive to it.

Check your weapons. Have you been in the Word like you were years ago? Have you been praying like you did several years ago? Have you experienced a little success in the Word of God and then laid it down? When problems begin compounding, engines start failing and things come apart, do you suddenly realize you don't have the kind of Word in your heart you thought you had? Has your commitment waned? Is your sensitivity to the Instructor (the Holy Spirit) what it should be?

Be sensitive to those in your midst who have just come out of training. Go back over your weapons with them. You may find out they remember what you may have forgotten.

Be sensitive to the entire Body of Christ. We have one goal ahead of us. It is not to prove who is the best "bomber pilot," the best preacher or the best wife. Our goal is to do our best and follow closely behind the Leader, the Lord Jesus Christ. Be sensitive to His command and meet the needs of this dying world. Pull Satan down from his strongholds.

CHAPTER SIX

Sensitivity
to Love

Sensitivity to Love

Become sensitive to the Holy Spirit Himself. God has sent His personal Emissary to lead and guide this great spiritual army.

Now is not the time to be so proud we can't be sensitive enough to the Holy Spirit to walk in love with our own husbands, wives, families or members of our crews. In World War II, each division had to cooperate with the other. Each service had its role to play. The war could not have been won without the joint operation of the Army, Navy, Air Force and Marine Corps all working together. In God's army, we are all fighting for the same cause. The Baptist unit, the Catholic unit, the Presbyterian unit, the Full Gospel unit will all have to work together. I am not going to miss the greatest spiritual outpouring this planet has ever seen over some minor, two-bit fuss that will never last in the light of God's power.

Ephesians 4:16 says, "From whom the whole body fitly joined together and compacted by that which every joint supplieth, according to the effectual working in the measure of every part, maketh increase of the body unto the edifying of itself in love." Jesus put the Body together, but the joints hold it together. If God is going to do anything about our unity, we have to do something about it. We are the ones who fail to stick together. Every part has its role to play.

The old adage that says, "A chain is only as strong as its weakest link," is true. When we find a weak link in the Body of Christ, we should not cut it off and criticize it. We should rally around the weak one and love him. We will carry him piggyback and strengthen him if we have to. We shouldn't be selfish.

Jesus put the Body together, but the joints hold it together.

We play a big part of the coming together in

the unity of our faith. God's influence will do it, but we have to agree with Him and become sensitive to His influence. "This I say therefore, and testify in the Lord, that ye henceforth walk not as other Gentiles walk, in the vanity of their mind, having the understanding darkened, being alienated from the life of God through the ignorance that is in them, because of the blindness [darkness, insensitiveness] of their heart" (Ephesians 4:17-18).

> *We play a big part of the coming together in the unity of our faith.*

It is possible to become insensitive, blind and hard, even though you are a born-again, Spirit-filled believer.

"Who being past feeling have given themselves over unto lasciviousness, to work all uncleanness with greediness" (verse 19). If the life of God is not flowing through your reborn spirit, lasciviousness will begin to work. Things you would not have done in the past don't look so bad anymore. *Lasciviousness* means "no restraint from impurity." The more insensitive you become, the less restraint you have to impurity.

Another way to say "impurity" is "weakness of the flesh." Your flesh cannot have the ascendancy over your spirit if you are practicing the Word of God. The Word builds sensitivity in your spirit to hear the voice of God. But the result of impurity will be the grieving of the Holy Spirit. If God is grieved, Jesus withdraws. He will never leave you, nor forsake you to the end of the earth, but if you are not sensitive to the Holy Spirit, you will find that when you *want* to hear Him, you can't. You think, *Dear God, I used to get all kinds of revelation. What's wrong?*

Do you remember how sensitive you were right after you were saved? You were in love with everyone but the devil! Then, perhaps a few people offended you, and you hardened yourself to them. It led you to judge them as hypocrites. Maybe you saw some humanity in ministers of God. You became disappointed by their lack of perfection.

No one has a right to judge any minister. He is not your servant. He is your gift. He is *God's* servant. Pray for him. Leave it up to God. You cannot judge another man's heart. There are two times when you ought to pray for someone. One is when you think he is right, the other is when you think he is wrong!

7

How to Develop Sensitivity

How to Develop Sensitivity

Making a quality decision to live the commandment of love is the beginning of a sensitive heart. A decision of quality is one from which there is no retreat and about which there is no more debate.

Love is tender. When I made the decision to walk in the commandment of love, I began to order my thinking in that direction and it softened my heart. This decision started the laws of the spirit working in my heart; causing it to be tender and sensitive.

Making a quality decision to live the commandment of love is the beginning of a sensitive heart.

I had to become sensitive to the commandment to walk in love when God called Gloria to preach. It was not easy to give up my cook! There are still people today whose opinion is, "Yes, women can pray. But bless God, they sure better clean house while they're doing it!"

I am not saying anyone ought to neglect their family. Everyone has duties in a household and must be sensitive to those duties. But, make it a point to be sensitive to the fact that other members of your family have things to do for God, too.

The hard part for me was dealing with my flesh. God had dealt with Gloria to pray in other tongues at least an hour every day. She gets up early and does it first thing every morning. I'm so grateful she prays! But I couldn't cope with why she didn't stop long enough to cook me some eggs. I was so insensitive. I thought it was more important for me to eat than for her to be in intercession for me, my life and ministry.

One morning I tore into the kitchen, slamming doors and banging pots around because I was angry. "Why won't she get in here and cook me some eggs?" I made the mistake of asking God. I said, "You called her to preach. Now what am I going to do about some eggs?" He said, *Cook them yourself.* That is not what I wanted to hear! It finally got to me that I was shameless and insensitive. I know what spiritual values are all about. She has saved my life more than once because of her tenacity about the Word of God.

I quickly started getting sensitive. I got on my knees and made a decision before Almighty God, and wrote it down. "I settle this forever before Almighty God. I will not listen to a lying spirit of the devil again. Self-pity, condemnation, self-debasement, unbelief and doubt have no more part in me, or I in them. I know how to receive, and how to please God, and I will do those things."

> *I made a decision to walk in love.*

I made a decision to walk in love. Then, my heart began to become tender and I began to act on what I knew to do. My thinking started to straighten out and instead of majoring in minors like insisting that Gloria cook, I began majoring in majors, like intercessory prayer.

Tenderness rose up on the inside of me. I made the decision to make this commandment of love the commandment of my life. I want to be someone with whom Jesus can have fun and share His life. I'm just barely beginning to get there. He's with me all the time, but there is something about being close to Him all the time. I don't want Him to withdraw from me because I'm insensitive.

Make the decision to live by faith. God is your source. You can't be sensitive to God and to others if you are always criticizing the government and those around you. Inflation and depression are not greater than the laws of God. Act on the laws of God when things get rough. Don't stop your giving, double up on it. Don't violate the laws of God, honor them and God will honor you.

Give the Word first place. Be sensitive to it. Whatever God's Word says, do it. If it says you are His righteousness—believe it. If it says you are healed—believe it. Walk in God's Word: Live it. Eat it. Sleep it. Study it. Meditate on it. Feed it into your heart and become sensitive to its every word.

Develop a personal relationship with God. Receive His Word as God speaking to *you.* Put your name in the promises. Talk to God as you talk to your closest friend. Be sensitive to enter in to praise and worship. It will cause you to be more sensitive to the Spirit of God, and more aware of His presence.

Then, get the sin out of your life. I made up my mind some time ago that I had been fighting some things long enough. There were some things in my life that needed purging. I separated myself to fast, pray and fellowship with God.

Fasting denies the flesh and allows your spirit to become more sensitive to God. It won't get the sin out of your life, but repentance will. I made up my mind I was not going to do anything else until all the sin was gone. I did what Joel 2:13 says: "Rend your heart, and not your garments." I opened my heart before God and I dug things out that I had been keeping hidden. I made the decision to do what it took to get the sin out of my life. I came out of there changed.

Walking in the spirit is walking with God, being sensitive and having a sensitive heart toward Him.

Finally, pray. Enter the life of the Spirit with all your heart, all your mind, all your strength and all your resources. Walking in the spirit is walking with God, being sensitive and having a sensitive heart toward Him.

CHAPTER EIGHT

Sensitivity
to Sacrifice

Sensitivity to Sacrifice

We are at war. Sacrifices are made during wartime that are not made at any other time. Sensitive wives release their husbands for battle. Sensitive parents release their sons and daughters.

World War II was fought when I was just a boy. I remember paper drives and rubber drives. We got involved any way we could. I was disappointed because I was too young to go fight. I wanted to give it everything I had. Everyone did. Wives, mothers and fathers willingly sacrificed loved ones to fight in that war. It was considered a privilege because we had a good cause to defend and a job that had to be done.

There will have to be many sacrifices made

in this war. Some young people will announce
to their parents that they won't be going to law
school or even to seminary. They will have
hearts sensitive enough to receive God's call to
go to "war"—dedicating their lives to taking
the delivering power of the gospel to their bud-
dies still on drugs. They will give up their own
plans and the plans of their parents, because
we are at war.

Some pastors will have to give up their local
respectability to be known as "holy rollers" and
"fanatics." Some will have to be sensitive
enough to go where the sinners are, instead of
expecting them to come to church.

To enter in to the spirit life of God, all areas
will have to be touched with sensi-

To enter in to the
spirit life of God,
all areas will
have to be
touched with
sensitivity.

tivity. Wives may tell their husbands
God has called them into a life of
intercession, or husbands may tell
their wives God has called them to
street ministry. It will take sensitivity
and sacrifices on everyone's part.

We will all have to be more sensitive to women in the ministry. The book of
Joel says that in the time of the outpouring,

everything the devil has taken will be replaced. The devil has stolen the ministry of our women away from us. Those ministries will be regenerated. Our sons *and* our daughters will prophesy. Before this outpouring is concluded, we will sit at the feet of some of the most powerful women of the ages. I am married to one of them, and I'm glad of it.

A woman, conducting herself properly, can minister to the Body of Christ like no man can. A man cannot preach from the viewpoint of a mother. God is as much a mother as He is a father. Adam was made in the image of God. He was as much female as he was male. He was exactly like God. Then God separated him and removed the female part. *Woman* means "man with the womb."[1] Eve had as much authority as Adam did, as long as they stayed together in agreement.

There is a dignity in a godly woman that is not in man. A man fathers a child, but God builds a depth of character into a woman that causes her to nurture and love the child she brings into this world. A woman has the dignity of God that no other thing created by God can portray.

Because of the Fall of man, woman was made to crawl under a curse. But, she has been redeemed from that curse (Galatians 3:13). Jesus has lifted womanhood to a place where the Bible says, "Children, obey your parents." It doesn't say, "Children, obey your father." The position of authority in a home is a man *and* a woman, *together* in agreement, being sensitive to one another, not making independent decisions.

There is not space here to give an in-depth explanation, but there are approximately 300 scriptures in the Bible proving women have an equal place with men in the ministry of the gospel. Become sensitive to the needs of the women in your life. Become sensitive to your wife, mother, daughter and the other women around you.

[1]Noah Webster, *An American Dictionary of the English Language,* Ninth Ed. [San Francisco: Foundation for American Christian Education, 1996] "woman"

CHAPTER NINE

Jesus Will Help You to Be Sensitive

Jesus Will Help You to Be Sensitive

If you don't know Jesus Christ as Lord and Savior, it is impossible to have a sensitive spirit. An unregenerate spirit is only full of woe and hate. You can't be sensitive and loving with a dead spirit. You could resolve to be loving and kind from now on and it wouldn't last because it is *not* the sensitivity of the Holy Spirit. The kind of sensitivity we are talking about is the life of God. The Bible says those who have blinded minds are alienated from the life of God (Ephesians 4:18).

Yet, through the new birth, God has promised to give you a new heart. Ezekiel 36:26-27 says, "A new heart also will I

The kind of sensitivity we are talking about is the life of God.

give you, and a new spirit will I put within you: and I will take away the stony heart out of your flesh, and I will give you an heart of flesh. And I will put my spirit within you, and cause you to walk in my statutes, and ye shall keep my judgments, and do them." A deep sensitivity will come and abide inside you. It is the very heart of God.

You will have a heart of flesh that can feel the deep sensations of the heart of God. When He is grieved, you will be grieved. When He is full of joy, you will be full of joy.

The life of God residing in your spirit is essential to your eternal salvation. Jesus said, "Whosoever believeth in him should not perish, but have eternal life" (John 3:15). His life in you is your assurance of victory in this life. "For whatsoever is born of God overcometh the world: and this is the victory that overcometh the world, even our faith. Who is he that overcometh the world, but he that believeth that Jesus is the Son of God?" (1 John 5:4-5).

You can overcome all the pressures and problems of the age we live in through Jesus Christ and sensitivity to His Spirit, His life and His compassion.

You can overcome all the pressures and problems of the age we live in through Jesus Christ and sensitivity to His Spirit, His life and His compassion abiding in you. You don't have to be defeated by inflation, depression, divorce, religious traditions, or sickness and disease. The Greater One dwells in you. "Ye are of God, little children, and have overcome them: because greater is he that is in you, than he that is in the world" (1 John 4:4).

If you do not know Jesus as your personal Lord and Savior, you can receive Him now. Join with me in praying this prayer. Don't just read it; make a conscious effort to speak these words from the very depths of your being. When you finish praying, you will be born again:

Heavenly Father, in the Name of Jesus, I present myself to You.

I pray and ask Jesus to be Lord over my life. I believe it in my heart, so I say it with my mouth: Jesus has been raised from the dead. This moment, I make Him the Lord over my life.

Jesus, come into my heart. I believe

that I am saved this moment. I believe that I am a child of Almighty God. I am reborn. I am a Christian. I believe that I have a sensitive heart and that I can know the very heartbeat of God.

I renounce sin, Satan and all he stands for. I renounce the past and look to Jesus for the future.

Now, I purpose to be sensitive to Your life and nature in my heart. By the help of the Holy Spirit, I will outwardly express the image of Jesus that I inwardly possess. Thank You for the power, the ability and the privilege, in Jesus' Name. Amen.

Prayer for Salvation and Baptism
in the Holy Spirit

Heavenly Father, I come to You in the Name of Jesus. Your Word says, "Whosoever shall call on the name of the Lord shall be saved" (Acts 2:21). I am calling on You. I pray and ask Jesus to come into my heart and be Lord over my life according to Romans 10:9-10: "If thou shalt confess with thy mouth the Lord Jesus, and shalt believe in thine heart that God hath raised him from the dead, thou shalt be saved. For with the heart man believeth unto righteousness; and with the mouth confession is made unto salvation." I do that now. I confess that Jesus is Lord, and I believe in my heart that God raised Him from the dead. I repent of sin. I renounce it. I renounce the devil and everything he stands for. Jesus is my Lord.

I am now reborn! I am a Christian—a child of Almighty God! I am saved! You also said in Your Word, "If ye then, being evil, know how to give good gifts unto your children: HOW MUCH MORE shall your heavenly Father give the Holy Spirit to them that ask him?" (Luke 11:13). I'm also asking You to fill me with the Holy Spirit. Holy Spirit, rise up within me as I praise God. I fully expect to speak with other tongues as You give me the utterance (Acts 2:4). In Jesus' Name. Amen!

Begin to praise God for filling you with the Holy Spirit. Speak those words and syllables you receive—not in your own language, but the language given to you by the Holy Spirit. You have to use your own voice. God will not force you to speak. Don't be concerned with how it sounds. It is a heavenly language!

Continue with the blessing God has given you and pray in the spirit every day.

You are a born-again, Spirit-filled believer. You'll never be the same!

Find a good church that boldly preaches God's Word and obeys it. Become part of a church family who will love and care for you as you love and care for them.

We need to be connected to each other. It increases our strength in God. It's God's plan for us.

Make it a habit to watch the Believer's Voice of Victory Network and become a doer of the Word, who is blessed in his doing (James 1:22-25).

About the Author

Kenneth Copeland is co-founder and president of Kenneth Copeland Ministries in Fort Worth, Texas, and best-selling author of books that include *Honor—Walking in Honesty, Truth and Integrity,* and *THE BLESSING of The LORD Makes Rich and He Adds No Sorrow With It.*

Since 1967, Kenneth has been a minister of the gospel of Christ and teacher of God's Word. He is also the artist on award-winning albums such as his Grammy-nominated *Only the Redeemed, In His Presence, He Is Jehovah, Just a Closer Walk* and *Big Band Gospel.* He also co-stars as the character Wichita Slim in the children's adventure videos *The Gunslinger, Covenant Rider* and the movie *The Treasure of Eagle Mountain,* and as Daniel Lyon in the Commander Kellie and the Superkids™ videos *Armor of Light* and *Judgment: The Trial of Commander Kellie.* Kenneth also co-stars as a Hispanic godfather in the 2009 and 2016 movies *The Rally* and *The Rally 2: Breaking the Curse.*

With the help of offices and staff in the United States, Canada, England, Australia, South Africa and Ukraine, Kenneth is fulfilling his vision to boldly preach the uncompromised WORD of God from the top of this world, to the bottom, and all the way around. His ministry reaches millions of people worldwide through daily and Sunday TV broadcasts, magazines, teaching audios and videos, conventions and campaigns, and the World Wide Web.

Learn more about Kenneth Copeland Ministries
by visiting our website at **kcm.org**

We're Here for You!®

Your growth in God's WORD and victory in Jesus are at the very center of our hearts. In every way God has equipped us, we will help you deal with the issues facing you, so you can be the **victorious overcomer** He has planned for you to be.

The mission of Kenneth Copeland Ministries is about all of us growing and going together. Our prayer is that you will take full advantage of all The LORD has given us to share with you.

Wherever you are in the world, you can watch the *Believer's Voice of Victory* broadcast on television (check your local listings), the Internet at kcm.org or on our digital Roku channel.

Our website, **kcm.org,** gives you access to every resource we've developed for your victory. And, you can find contact information for our international offices in Africa, Australia, Canada, Europe, Ukraine and our headquarters in the United States.

Each office is staffed with devoted men and women, ready to serve and pray with you. You can contact the worldwide office nearest you for assistance, and you can call us for prayer at our U.S. number, 1-817-852-6000, seven days a week!

We encourage you to connect with us often and let us be part of your everyday walk of faith!

Jesus Is LORD!

Kenneth & Gloria Copeland

Kenneth and Gloria Copeland